T0375074

HEBREWS

RACE TO
GLORY

JAMES
REAPSOME

13 STUDIES
FOR INDIVIDUALS
OR GROUPS

ivp

Life
Builder
Study

INTER-VARSITY PRESS
36 Causton Street, London SW1P 4ST, England
Email: ivp@ivpbooks.com
Website: www.ivpbooks.com

Originally published in the United States of America in the LifeGuide® Bible Studies series in 2001 by InterVarsity Press, Downers Grove, Illinois
First published in Great Britain by Scripture Union in 2003
This edition published in Great Britain by Inter-Varsity Press 2018

British Library Cataloguing-in-Publication Data
A catalogue record for this book is available from the British Library.

ISBN: 978–1–78359–779–6

Printed in Great Britain by Ashford Colour Press Ltd, Gosport, Hampshire

Inter-Varsity Press publishes Christian books that are true to the Bible and that communicate the gospel, develop discipleship and strengthen the church for its mission in the world.

IVP originated within the Inter-Varsity Fellowship, now the Universities and Colleges Christian Fellowship, a student movement connecting Christian Unions in universities and colleges throughout Great Britain, and a member movement of the International Fellowship of Evangelical Students. Website: www.uccf.org.uk. That historic association is maintained, and all senior IVP staff and committee members subscribe to the UCCF Basis of Faith.

Contents

Getting the Most
Out of *Hebrews*

A former Olympic distance runner and veteran missionary wrote the following to a friend who was caught in the throes of a horrendous personal crisis:

> In this race . . . I suddenly hit a branch of a tree (and) . . . the blow almost knocked me out. . . . It knocked me out of my race, stopped me cold. . . . Somehow I staggered back on the track and stumbled along. . . . I remember one clear conclusion. I must keep going, even if I come in long behind. I must not quit. So I kept going. I won the race. . . .
>
> Whatever the difficulty, the blow, we must keep on. God will lead to the result that will glorify him.*

The sentence "Whatever . . . the blow, we must keep on" captures the theme of the letter to the Hebrews, which I have entitled *Race to Glory*. The author of Hebrews states it very clearly: "Let us run with perseverance the race marked out for us" (12:1).

Throughout, the author emphasizes this chief concern for the readers—that they finish their faith race with Jesus Christ gloriously and triumphantly. "Pay more careful attention," the author warns, "so that we do not drift away" (2:1). "Let us be careful that none of you be found to have fallen short of [God's promised rest]" (4:1). "Let us leave the elementary teachings about Christ and go on to maturity," the writer appeals (6:1). "We want each of you to show this same diligence to the very end, in order to make your hope sure" (6:11).

After convincingly showing how Jesus Christ meets all of our needs, the writer cries out, "Let us draw near to God with a sincere heart in full assurance of faith. . . . Let us hold unswervingly to the hope we profess, for he who promised is faithful" (10:22-23). "Do not throw away your confidence. . . . You need to persevere so that when you have done the will of God, you will receive what he has promised" (10:35-36).

The author devotes an entire chapter (11) to drawing the readers to the stories of great heroes who finished the race to glory, people like Moses, Abraham, Noah, Jacob and Joseph. These witnesses are summoned to inspire us onward in our own faith race.

A friend of mine loves to joke that when he gets to heaven he is going to find out who wrote Hebrews. The letter bears no byline, so scholars have had a field day speculating about its possible authors. Included in this list are Paul, Silas, Titus, Mark, Clement, Luke, Aquila, Priscilla and Barnabas. If you took a poll among these scholars, Luke, Barnabas and Apollos would be strongly favored. At any rate, whoever the author was, he or she knew the Hebrews very well.

The readers were knowledgeable Jews who had converted to faith in Jesus Christ. The entire scaffolding of the letter is Jewish history, theology and practice. These Jews were old enough in the faith to be teachers and to recall older leaders (5:12; 13:7). They had served one another and had suffered (6:10; 10:32-34). Their city can only be guessed at—possibly Jerusalem, Alexandria, Corinth, Ephesus or Rome.

What is clear about the audience is their spiritual peril. They were in danger of reverting to Judaism. The letter is chock full of warnings about it. They were being taunted by Jews as apostates from God and renegades from Moses. They were accused of abandoning their law and forfeiting the Old Testament promises.

So the writer goes to great lengths to prove that Jesus Christ is far superior to everything they had left behind for his sake. In that context he warns them against neglect, unbelief, disobedience, immaturity and rejection. He stands in the grandstand, as it were, wildly cheering them on to stay on the track, to not quit and to reach the finish line in the power of Jesus Christ.

Today's readers most likely will not have come to faith in Christ out of such a deeply embedded cultural and religious tradition. But every Christian at some time or other is tempted to quit and to ask, "What's the use?" As problems and roadblocks mount, as faith seems unproductive, as doors slam, we find it easy to think about quitting our personal faith race.

We also need current reminders about the supremacy of Jesus Christ. There is no stronger enticement to stay in the race than to "fix your eyes on Jesus" (12:2). As the pioneer of our salvation, he brings us to glory (2:10).

We run our faith race in vital communion with God through prayer, by giving God's Word command of our lives, by faithfully worshiping him and loving fellow Christians, and by knowing and serving Jesus Christ better each day as our daily companion, guide and master.

Suggestions for Individual Study

1. As you begin each study, pray that God will speak to you through his Word.

2. Read the introduction to the study and respond to the personal reflection question or exercise. This is designed to help you focus on God and on the theme of the study.

3. Each study deals with a particular passage—so that you can delve into the author's meaning in that context. Read and reread the passage to be studied. If you are studying a book, it will be helpful to read through the entire book prior to the first study. The questions are written using the language of the New International Version, so you may wish to use that version of the Bible. The New Revised Standard Version is also recommended.

4. This is an inductive Bible study, designed to help you discover for yourself what Scripture is saying. The study includes three types of questions. *Observation* questions ask about the basic facts: who, what, when, where and how. *Interpretation* questions delve into the meaning of the passage. *Application* questions help you discover the implications of the text for growing in Christ. These three keys unlock the treasures of Scripture.

Write your answers to the questions in the spaces provided or in a personal journal. Writing can bring clarity and deeper understanding of yourself and of God's Word.

5. It might be good to have a Bible dictionary handy. Use it to look up any unfamiliar words, names or places.

6. Use the prayer suggestion to guide you in thanking God for what you have learned and to pray about the applications that have come to mind.

7. You may want to go on to the suggestion under "Now or Later," or you may want to use that idea for your next study.

Suggestions for Members of a Group Study

1. Come to the study prepared. Follow the suggestions for individual study mentioned above. You will find that careful preparation will greatly enrich your time spent in group discussion.

2. Be willing to participate in the discussion. The leader of your group will not be lecturing. Instead, he or she will be encouraging the members of the group to discuss what they have learned. The leader will be asking the questions that are found in this guide.

3. Stick to the topic being discussed. Your answers should be based on the verses which are the focus of the discussion and not on outside authorities such as commentaries or speakers. These studies focus on a particular passage of Scripture. Only rarely should you refer to other portions of the Bible. This allows for everyone to participate in in-depth study on equal ground.

4. Be sensitive to the other members of the group. Listen attentively when they describe what they have learned. You may be surprised by their insights! Each question assumes a variety of answers. Many questions do not have "right" answers, particularly questions that aim at meaning or application. Instead the questions push us to explore the passage more thoroughly.

When possible, link what you say to the comments of others. Also, be affirming whenever you can. This will encourage some of the more hesitant members of the group to participate.

5. Be careful not to dominate the discussion. We are sometimes so eager to express our thoughts that we leave too little opportunity for others to respond. By all means participate! But allow others to also.

6. Expect God to teach you through the passage being discussed and through the other members of the group. Pray that you will have an enjoyable and profitable time together, but also that as a result of the study you will find ways that you can take action individually and/or as a group.

7. Remember that anything said in the group is considered confidential and should not be discussed outside the group unless specific permission is given to do so.

8. If you are the group leader, you will find additional suggestions at the back of the guide.

---

[*]Cited in Gordon MacDonald, *Rebuilding Your Broken World* (Nashville: Oliver-Nelson, 1988), p. 224.

1

Starting the Race

Hebrews 1

According to legend, John Chrysostom, bishop of Constantinople (d. 407), was summoned by the ruler and threatened with banishment if he did not renounce Jesus Christ. Chrysostom responded, "You cannot banish me, for the whole world is my Father's kingdom."

"Then I will take away your life," said the emperor.

"You cannot," answered Chrysostom, "for my life is hid with Christ in God."

"I will take away your treasure," roared the emperor.

"You can't," replied Chrysostom, "for my treasure is in heaven, where my heart is."

"Then I will drive you away from all your friends," the emperor said.

"You cannot, for I have one friend from whom you can never separate me. I defy you," said Chrysostom, "because you can do me no harm."

Such conviction grows out of a firm grasp of who Jesus Christ really is.

GROUP DISCUSSION. "Christ, Buddha, Muhammad, they're all alike," someone tells you. What do you say?

PERSONAL REFLECTION. What have been the significant steps in your growing understanding of the person and work of Christ?

The writer of Hebrews will get you started in the race with an astounding look at the majesty, power and glory of Jesus Christ. *Read Hebrews 1.*

1. What do verses 1-3 reveal about who Christ is and what he was to accomplish?

2. What difference does it make that God "has spoken to us by his Son" (v. 2)?

3. How do you feel about how Jesus relates to us in light of this passage?

4. Because there are so many aspects to who Christ is, we may find ourselves responding to him in different ways at different times. Compare and contrast your response to Christ as Creator and Sustainer to Christ as the one who provided the only remedy for our sins.

5. What assurance about Christ's work of purification of our sins do we receive from the fact that he now sits at the Father's right hand?

6. To drive his point home, the author uses seven Old Testament citations. What characteristics or attributes of Jesus does the writer find in the Old Testament to prove his claim that Jesus is superior to angels (vv. 4-14)?

_____

7. Why do you think angels are contrasted with Jesus in this way?

_____

8. What do these quotes tell us about the authority of our Old Testament?

_____

9. Based on what you have observed in this passage, how would you answer the question "Who is Christ?"

_____

10. What needs in your life do these qualities of Jesus address?

_____

11. What kind of life should you have because all this is true of Jesus?

Pray that your life will increasingly reveal your growing appreciation of Christ's superiority and supremacy.

Now or Later

Plan to spend time thinking through the implications of Christ's supremacy in the context of our society's "it's all good" values.

2

Warning Signs

"Warning!" A black-and-white-lettered sign that I encounter on the Fox River in St. Charles, Illinois, warns me of a dam ahead. In that placid stream it would be easy to drift over the dam. Cigarette packs, cans of weed killer, fences around nuclear power plants—they all carry impressive warnings, designed to steer us from life-threatening perils. At an amusement park a child was killed because her mother ignored the warning about the age and height requirements. Rookie pro football players sleep through a lecture warning them about the dangers of alcohol abuse.

We resist warnings because we think they inhibit our freedoms. The Bible reveals that God gives us fair warnings about the risks and dangers that lie ahead in our faith race.

GROUP DISCUSSION. "Now you listen to me, you hear!" You may have heard this complaint from a parent, a teacher or even a drill sergeant. Similarly, Jesus struggled with different groups of people who heard and heard and heard (Mark 4:1-20) but produced nothing. What causes spiritual indifference?

PERSONAL REFLECTION. How can I grow more sensitive to God's voice giving me the best warnings and directions for my life?

In Hebrews 2, the writer erects the first of six prominent warning signs in the letter. The first, in effect, alerts us to the danger of drifting off the course of our faith race. It tells us to concentrate on staying in the race. *Read Hebrews 2.*

---

1. In verse 1 we read, "pay more careful attention . . . to," and in verse 3 we are told not to "ignore." What is it that we are to focus our lives on?

---

2. What might cause you to "drift away" from Christ, or to let "such a great salvation" slip away like a loose ring that falls off your finger?

---

3. What logic does the writer use in verses 2-3 to further focus our attention on the peril of drifting away?

---

4. How does the writer strengthen the warning that God's salvation in Christ is well worth our most intense obedience (vv. 3-4)?

---

5. What helps you to maintain a warm, life-changing relationship with Jesus?

---

6. To prove that Jesus is too great and too valuable to neglect, the writer tells us more about him (vv. 5-9). What major facts does he cite here?

7. From the description of Jesus in verses 10-13, paint a picture of him that would encourage another Christian today.

8. Why did Jesus have "to be made like his brothers [you and me] in every way" (vv. 16-18)?

9. How does Jesus help you when you are tempted?

10. If you were to give Jesus names or titles based on verses 5-18, what would they be?

How does knowing these titles or roles of Jesus keep you from drifting away from him and staying in the faith race?

11. "Be sure your seatbelts are securely fastened," the aircraft's captain warns you because of approaching turbulence. How can you help one another to be "securely fastened" into Jesus?

Ask God to show you some steps you can take to keep anchored to Christ.

Now or Later
Reflect on some experiences that have drawn you away from Christ. What influenced your decisions in these matters?

3

Winning the Race

Coaches tell us that what distinguishes average from superior athletes is the will to win. Endowed with equal physical strengths, one reaches the heights of stardom while the other slips into obscurity.

In this chapter, the writer describes two equally endowed Christian runners in the faith race. One succeeded and the other failed. What made the difference? The will to win. One held firmly to Christ, but the other fell by the wayside because of a hard heart.

GROUP DISCUSSION. What makes the difference between vibrant, growing Christians you know and those who appear to be dull and uninterested in the implications of their profession of faith?

PERSONAL REFLECTION. Think about what motivates you to develop strong spiritual muscles and the will to win. What goals do you want to reach? Why?

By this time we know how seriously the writer views the perils of our faith race. He plunges into Old Testament history to make his warning even stronger. *Read Hebrews 3.*

---

1. What does the writer emphasize about Jesus in verses 1-6 that would encourage us to "fix [our] thoughts" on him (v. 1) and "hold on" to our courage and hope (v. 6)?

2. Why would it be essential for the Hebrews to be convinced that Jesus is greater than Moses (vv. 2-6)?

3. How do you concentrate intensely on Jesus (v. 1), especially when you are being tested by adversity, neglect or indifference?

4. In verses 7-11 the writer hoists his second warning—unbelief and disobedience. These verses describe the nation of Israel after they crossed the Red Sea. They refused to obey God's command to take the Promised Land because they were afraid of the military might they would face. So they were forced to wander forty years till that whole generation died off. How does the psalmist describe God's perspective on the Israelites?

5. In what ways might Christians "test and try" God (v. 9)? Why?

6. How do people act whose hearts have turned away from God?

7. Why do we need encouragement every day to hold fast to Christ?

8. How did God judge the Israelites whom Moses led out of Egypt (vv. 15-19)?

Why did he judge them in this way?

9. How seriously do you think Christians today take disobedience and unbelief? Explain.

10. On the positive side, what advantages are given to the one who has the will to win the race and who shares in all that Christ offers (v. 14)?

11. Review the facts about the hardhearted (vv. 8, 10, 12-13, 15-18). Which aspects of this lifestyle come closest to your experience?

12. What are you doing to avoid the peril of "falling in the desert" (v. 17)?

Thank God for his saving grace and for his forgiveness of your sins through your faith in Christ. Ask him to protect you from a hard heart.

Now or Later

Make your own list of qualities that separate people with hard hearts from those with faithful, believing hearts. Then list the names of those whose examples you would like to follow. What do you have to do to get moving?

4

Receiving God's Blessings

Hebrews 4:1-13

American financial statistician Roger Babson once observed, "Opportunities are greater today than ever before in history. Young people have greater chances for health, happiness, and prosperity than had the children of any previous generation."* The same is true for Christians in God's faith race.

GROUP DISCUSSION. Why do you think some Christians miss out on the chance to find God's richest blessings?

PERSONAL REFLECTION. Rate your satisfaction with your Christian life and faith on a scale of 1-10. What impediments must be removed? What new qualities added?

This chapter tells Christians in the race that there is something to fear but also something to strive for—experiencing God's promised rest now. *Read Hebrews 4:1-13.*

---

1. We are told to do our best to reach God's rest (3:11, 18; 4:1, 3, 5-6, 9-11). How do you picture such rest?

2. What do you think the promise of entering God's rest means in verse 1?

3. The tragic fate of the Israelites who perished in the desert serves as the basis of God's warning to those who have heard the gospel. Why did some who had the gospel preached to them miss their opportunity to receive God's rest (v. 2)?

4. From what you have observed in Hebrews thus far, how would you describe the faith that is required to receive God's rest?

5. God rested from all of his work (v. 4), and he offers us a "Sabbath-rest" on the seventh day of the week. What does it mean to you to rest from your work?

6. Verses 6-8 refer to the Israelites. How did they refuse to receive God's rest?

7. The "word of God" that judges our thoughts and attitudes (vv. 12-13) is the specific promise of God's rest. How can God's Word show you the condition of your heart?

8. How should our exposure to God's scrutiny and our accountability to him affect our thoughts and attitudes (v. 13)?

---

9. What role does Scripture have in your life now?

How would you like to deepen or change that relationship?

---

10. What would being able to experience God's rest mean to your life right now?

Pray that God will enlarge your vision of all that he has to give you in Christ.

Now or Later

Take time to think about your worries. List the categories: health, work, marriage and so on. Ask God to help you overcome them in the light of his provision of rest for your soul.

---

*Jacob M. Braude, *New Treasury of Stories for Every Speaking and Writing Occasion* (Englewood Cliffs, N.J.: Prentice-Hall, 1959), p. 255.

5

Overcoming Weakness

The Pulitzer Prize-winning book *City of Joy* tells about the intense suffering of a Polish priest in a Calcutta slum. His superiors offered him a comfortable lodging, but he chose to live just like the slum-dwellers. By his suffering he learned what it was like to be a slum-dweller. He could not have learned that any other way.

GROUP DISCUSSION. In what ways does our culture isolate us from the weaknesses of others?

How can we resist being desensitized to the massive needs around the world?

PERSONAL REFLECTION. What experiences have you had that have helped you to better understand another person?

The Hebrews needed to be reminded of their God-appointed, suffering high priest, Jesus Christ, so they would hold firmly to him. But the writer says they had to grow up from spiritual infancy. After his warnings against unbelief and missing God's rest, the writer returns to his theme of Jesus Christ, our great high priest (2:17; 3:1). *Read Hebrews 4:14—5:10.*

1. What do you learn about Jesus from these verses?

2. What commands are given in 4:14 and 16?

When is this difficult for you?

3. What is there about the character of Jesus that encourages us to obey these commands?

4. When you are tempted, what difference does it make to know that Jesus was likewise tempted and therefore sympathizes with your weakness?

5. Jesus, as our merciful and faithful high priest, made atonement for our sins. The writer reminds the Hebrews of their earthly high priest in Judaism. What was the high priest like (5:1-4)?

6. What main fact does the author establish about the high priesthood of Jesus (5:5)?

What difference does it make?

7. How would you compare Jesus' high appointment with the life he lived (5:7-8)?

8. How does your life reflect your high appointment as the adopted son or daughter of God?

9. What was the result of Christ's suffering (5:8-10)?

10. How does this help you to take a positive attitude toward suffering?

11. In what ways does your obedience to Christ transform hardship into spiritual growth and perseverance?

Thank and praise Jesus for his sympathy for all your needs and circumstances.

Now or Later

Think through the theme of Christ's "reverential submission" (5:7). What steps can you take to follow his example?

6

The Race
to Maturity

Peter Snell, former Olympic gold medalist, said that the only way to win a race is to get in front and go flat out. Prior to that, he said, it takes a whole lot of hard training and self-discipline.

GROUP DISCUSSION. What moral and spiritual qualities are required to win a gold medal in God's faith race? Why? How can we develop these qualities?

PERSONAL REFLECTION. When are you most tempted to drop out of the faith race? Why?

The Hebrews were in desperate danger of quitting the race, so the writer urged them to go forward. This is a chapter with four strong appeals: "Let us go on to maturity" (v. 1), "Show . . . diligence" (v. 11), "Do not . . . become lazy" (v. 12), "Take hold of the hope" (v. 18). *Read Hebrews 5:11—6:20.*

---

1. How would you describe the failures of the Hebrews?

2. In view of their resources and opportunities for growth, how do you account for their problems?

3. Why is "infant" (5:13) an apt description of spiritual failure?

4. The foundation of our Christian faith is essential, but what were the Hebrews doing (6:1-3)?

5. According to 6:4-6, why is it absolutely essential to develop Christian maturity?

6. What are the consequences of falling by the wayside (so to speak)?

7. Two kinds of land production vividly portray the reason to go on to maturity (6:7-8). How does each characterize your life?

8. What hope does the writer see for better things to come (6:9-10)? Why?

9. As you reflect on your track record of both diligence and laziness (6:11-12), how can you improve?

10. What essential part of God's nature encourages the Hebrews to be positive and hopeful about their future (6:13-18)?

11. How would you describe the anchor of your soul (6:19)?

12. In 6:19-20 the writer returns to the Hebrews' familiar religion of priests and their temple with its holy place curtained off. In other words, it was a picture of a more profound spiritual reality in Christ. How does Jesus fulfill your deepest aspirations and help you to go on to maturity in your faith race?

Thank God for his faithful warnings. Pray for discipline to be realistic but not to dwell on negatives. Focus your praise on what Jesus has done for you.

Now or Later

List all the dangers you face that could lead you off the track. Across the page in another column, list all the advantages you have in Christ, your church and your community to keep you pursuing your goal of faithful obedience to Christ.

7

Eternal
Companion

In the Old Testament, religion and priests went hand in hand. Moses had carefully laid out all the rules for the Levites, the priestly clan of Israel. When they began following Christ, the Hebrew Christians had departed from their old religion that was centered on priestly functions. Yet some of them hankered to return to their old ways. "Don't turn back," the writer appeals. "You have something far better in Christ."

GROUP DISCUSSION. Given that many people do not have strong religious traditions, what standards of judgment do people use to determine their faith and values?

PERSONAL REFLECTION. "He always makes me feel so strong," a church member said of the pastor after a sermon. What relationships strengthen your knowledge of Christ and build you up?

Regardless of whether we have had to move away from old traditions to find Christ, we all need confidence builders like chapter 7 so that as we run our faith race, we will stick with Jesus no matter what. *Read Hebrews 7.*

---

1. Jesus is our high priest, not of the ancient Jewish line of Aaron, but of Melchizedek. "Just think how great he [Melchizedek] was," commands the writer (v. 4). What made Melchizedek so great (vv. 1-3)?

2. The Hebrew patriarch Abraham tithed (gave one-tenth of his income) to Melchizedek (v. 4). According to verses 5-10, why does this prove that Jesus' high priesthood is superior to that of Levi (Aaron's son)?

3. Jesus inaugurated a new era because he was not of the priestly tribe (vv. 11-14). On what does his priestly authority rest (vv. 15-17)?

4. How can Jesus' everlastingness affect your day-to-day ups and downs?

5. In what sense were the rules of the Jews "weak and useless" (vv. 18-19)?

6. Why is our hope in Christ a "better hope" (v. 19)?

7. God's oath set aside Jesus as a distinctive high priest (vv. 20-21). How does Jesus guarantee our faith agreement (covenant) with him (v. 22)?

8. What does the permanence of Christ's priesthood make possible for us (vv. 23-25)?

---

9. How does Jesus' nonstop prayer for you help you to hold firmly to your faith and persevere in the race (v. 25)?

---

10. What about Christ's character and sacrifice sets him far above other earthly priests (vv. 26-28)?

---

11. Twice the writer tells us to come to God through Christ's high priesthood (vv. 19, 25). Why do we need to do this?

How can you practice it in your faith race?

As you pray, thank God for all of the qualities of Jesus you can think of, and praise him for meeting your needs.

Now or Later

How does the work of Jesus on the cross deal with your past, present and future sins?

8

God's "New Deal"

Hebrews 8

Back in the 1930s, President Franklin Roosevelt sought to rescue the country from the pit of the Great Depression by launching the New Deal. The concept caught the imagination of the people; the time was ripe for a radically new economic and social program.

GROUP DISCUSSION. How are the concepts of "new," "improved" and "better" used in advertising?

Why are they effective?

PERSONAL REFLECTION. How are you growing in relationships that will help you to demonstrate that you have new life in Christ?

In this chapter, the writer of Hebrews announces God's "new deal"—a covenant, or agreement, between God and humanity. It offers far superior promises to those of the "old deal" (Old Testament laws and regulations). *Read Hebrews 8.*

---

1. "We do have such a high priest" (v. 1) refers to the description of Jesus in 7:23-28. What additional facts do you learn about him (vv. 1-2)?

2. What is Christ's heavenly ministry (vv. 3-6)?

3. How do you respond to this picture of Christ?

4. Verse 6 looks back to prove Christ's superior ministry and forward to prove that we have a superior covenant with God. The key is "better promises." What was the problem with the first covenant (vv. 7-12)?

5. What are the main benefits for us of God's "new deal"?

6. Do you function better under external restraint (the law) or inner constraint (God's Spirit) (v. 10)? Why?

7. What is one purpose of God's new plan (v. 10)?

8. The distinctive mark of God's children is that they know him (v. 11). How does such knowledge transform your life?

9. What guarantees God's "new deal" (v. 12; see also vv. 1-3; 9:14)?

10. How is the covenant promise of forgiveness better than the old covenant?

11. What happens to you when you say to God, "Thank you for forgiving and forgetting my sin"?

12. A magazine ad for dishwashers offers more power, more pizzazz and more performance. How could your understanding and application of God's "new deal" offer all of that to you in your walk with him?

Thank God that according to his grace in Christ you do not need to keep a host of rules and regulations in order to enjoy the fruits of your salvation.

Now or Later

The writer uses the Old Testament to buttress his arguments. Plan to take some extra study time to learn why this was so important. In what ways can your studies of the Old Testament help you to grow in Christ?

9

The Runner's Power

Hebrews 9

In view of the colossal problems besetting us—drugs, divorce, depression, to name a few—it seems like a gross oversimplification to say that the blood of Jesus Christ is the solution. But in a different context, the Hebrews faced similar problems of neglect, unbelief and immaturity. They were in danger of dropping out of the race and turning back to their old ways. Seemingly, they lacked the power and purpose to advance and press on in their faith race.

GROUP DISCUSSION. Why does our culture often deny and dodge the truth of Christ—that he offered his own blood for humanity's sins?

PERSONAL REFLECTION. Think about your first experience reading the account of Christ's Passion week. How did it affect you? Why? Why is it important to keep reading the story?

What was the solution given to the Hebrews? The blood of Jesus. Only a full and perfect knowledge of what Jesus is and does for us can bring us to a full and perfect Christian life. *Read Hebrews 9.*

1. Describe the Old Testament sanctuary from verses 1-5. (What did it look like? What would it have felt like to be there?)

2. What was the point of the reminders about the Old Testament sanctuary (vv. 1-5)?

3. In what way did the priests' gifts and sacrifices fall short (vv. 6-10)?

4. Contrast what Jesus did (vv. 11-14) with the old system (vv. 1-10). How could you successfully marshal a debate to show that Jesus came to give us something better?

5. In verse 15 "for this reason" introduces the writer's proof of why Jesus had to offer his blood for us. What does it mean to you that you are set free to receive an eternal inheritance?

6. Why was the shedding of sacrificial blood required even under the old covenant (vv. 16-22)?

7. The writer explains why the offering of Jesus' blood is not only necessary but also a superior sacrifice. Why is it important to direct our attention to "heavenly things" (v. 23)?

8. In what sense was Jesus qualified "to appear for us in God's presence" (v. 24)?

9. What difference would it make to those steeped in Old Testament religion to know that Jesus once-for-all offered his own blood, rather than offering animal blood (vv. 25-26)?

10. How can you deepen your understanding of and appreciation for Christ's self-sacrifice?

11. How would you encourage someone to face eternity with hope and peace, based on what you have learned in this chapter?

12. Also certain is Jesus' second coming (v. 28). In light of his blood offering, how would you like to spend your time waiting for him?

Thank and praise the Lord Jesus Christ for his suffering to make atonement for your sins. Be specific about the benefits of his death for you.

Now or Later

Think about people you know who find Christ's blood to be offensive. How can you pray for them? What can you do to introduce them to Jesus?

10

Staying in the Race

Faced with seemingly eternal years of schoolwork and a multitude of rules to obey, children get discouraged. When that happens, parents say, "Look at your great opportunities. Take advantage of what you have now. Don't throw it away."

GROUP DISCUSSION. Recall an opportunity you missed because it sounded too good. What did you miss by not believing the evidence?

PERSONAL REFLECTION. Confess times when you've wasted opportunities for spiritual growth and development. Think about possible reasons for your failure. What encouragement does Hebrews have to offer you?

The writer of Hebrews, in chapter 10, reaches the heights of Mount Everest with a picture of Jesus that offers his readers encouragement. From those lofty heights he tells them to warm up to God, hold their faith in him, and stir up one another in Christian faith and practice. His argument culminates at 10:18; it seems that he can gather no further evidence to draw them back to Jesus. *Read Hebrews 10.*

---

1. How do verses 1-4 prove that the Old Testament system was a shadow, not the real thing?

2. Contrast Jesus' sacrifice (the reality) with the shadow (vv. 5-10). Why is his sacrifice better?

3. What did he do for us that the Old Testament sacrifices could not (vv. 10, 14)?

4. As you meditate on verses 11-18 and the awesome love and power of Jesus to take away your sins, what are the responses in your heart and mind?

5. Summarize what God wants to do for you in Christ (vv. 1-2, 4, 10-11, 14-15, 17-18).

What could you do if you don't feel "holy" or "perfect"?

6. In light of what God has done for us in Christ (vv. 19-21), what three commands does the writer feel compelled to issue (vv. 22-24)?

7. What does the awesome privilege of coming close to God mean for us (v. 22)?

8. What role do others play in helping us to "hold unswervingly" to our faith (v. 23-25)?

9. If we fail to draw near to God, hold fast our faith and stir up one another, what is likely to happen (vv. 25-26, 38-39)?

10. How does the writer make clear that his warning of punishment applies to professing Christians (vv. 30-34)?

11. What purposes could be achieved in your life by both this strong encouragement and this stern warning?

Look at verses 11-18 again, and look for facts for which you can be thankful to God. Praise him in quietness and confidence.

Now or Later
During the past week, what thoughts crossed your mind about quitting your faith race? List the pros and cons. What convinced you to keep following Jesus?

How can you help someone this week who is struggling to keep the faith?

11

Models of Faith

Probably no subject is so glibly misunderstood as faith. Nearly everyone professes to have some of it. Many people would like to have more.

GROUP DISCUSSION. Complete the sentence: "Faith is . . ."

PERSONAL REFLECTION. Pretend you are making a spreadsheet of your faith account. What are your assets? your liabilities? What is the bottom line today?

The writer to the Hebrews takes faith out of religious theory and clothes it with flesh and blood. The author does this with what we today call role models. These models inspire us to go on believing in Jesus. The writer gives an awesome array of examples of faith recorded in Scripture. *Read Hebrews 11.*

1. How can you be sure of your hopes and be certain of what you can't see (v. 1)?

2. What else does faith enable us to do (vv. 3, 6)?

3. Look for both assured confidence and calm expectation (v. 1) in the role models of faith in this chapter. How did Abel, Enoch and Noah express their faith (vv. 4-7)?

4. Considering the foolishness of Abraham's choices by human standards, what do you think his emotions were like (vv. 8-10)?

In what way would his hope for "the city without foundations" enable him to endure?

5. What unseen certainties have guided you in making fundamental, life-changing decisions?

6. What subtle irony about the power of faith comes out in verse 12?

7. How does the promise of a heavenly country help us to keep our faith, even when we don't see our hopes fulfilled immediately (vv. 13-16)?

8. Why do you think Abraham's faith triumphed when he was asked to give up Isaac (vv. 17-19)?

9. How would you compare the faith of the named heroes and heroines who achieved greatness (vv. 20-35) with those unnamed persons who suffered grievously (vv. 35-38)?

10. Some Christians believe that faith always leads to material and physical blessing. What does this passage tell you about the role of both blessing and suffering for the faithful?

11. In tough circumstances, what connection do you make between your faith and the certainty of resurrection (v. 35)?

12. What has God enabled you to do through faith?

Thank God for each person he has used in your life to help you to faith in Christ.

Now or Later

Make your own contemporary list of heroes and heroines of faith. Why are they included? What part did they play in your life? Can you be a model of faith to someone else? How?

12

The Runner's Discipline

Hebrews 12

We often wonder why thousands of marathoners seem to enjoy punishing themselves in those grueling races. Certainly, for most, it's not the hope of winning. What is it then? Explaining it to his readers, writer Art Carey said, "The real joy of the Boston Marathon is just finishing, just winning the contest with yourself—doing what you have set out to do."*

GROUP DISCUSSION. Why is perseverance usually not at the top of the list of the qualities we most admire in people?

PERSONAL REFLECTION. What are your faith-race goals?

This chapter focuses on the disciplines of faith. Like the heroes mentioned in chapter 11, believers are called to stay in the faith race until the end. *Read Hebrews 12.*

1. What hindrances and entanglements get in the way of your Christian faith race (v. 1)? Why?

2. Up to this point in the letter, how has the writer encouraged perseverance by pointing to Jesus?

3. What value is it to keep your eyes on Jesus (vv. 2-3)?

How do you accomplish this?

4. What discipline of the Hebrews do you think the writer alludes to (vv. 3-4, 7; 11:35-38)?

5. How do the values of God's discipline cited here help us to respond positively to discipline (vv. 10-12)?

6. How have you been able to "strengthen your feeble arms and weak knees" when under discipline (v. 12)?

7. Identify the writer's specific instructions in verses 14-17.

What principles are they based on?

8. How could you identify a "bitter root" or a "godless Esau" in your life (vv. 15-16)?

---

9. What encouragement do you find in verses 18-24 to run the faith race with perseverance?

---

10. We've all been tempted to drop out of the race. Why would the warning of verses 25-29 cause us to reconsider?

---

11. In what ways does your worship reflect (or fail to reflect) the fact that God is a "consuming fire" (v. 29)?

Fixing your eyes on Jesus, confess your sins. Ask him for the determination to keep following him, regardless of the cost.

Now or Later

What circumstances feel like a spiritual marathon in your life?

What can you do this week to regain your strength and resolve to keep running your faith race? Look for help in your church and community.

---

*Art Carey, *The Philadelphia Inquirer,* April 23, 1978.

13

Running by the Rules

Hebrews 13

Ben Johnson of Canada was stripped of the Olympic gold medals he won at Seoul in 1988 because he broke the rules about drug use. Similarly, the Christian's faith race is much more than a sprint to the finish line. It's a race that brings glory to God by the way the runners behave.

GROUP DISCUSSION. How do you account for the attitude among some Christians who apparently think that it does not matter how they live, as long as they are "saved" or "belong to the church"?

PERSONAL REFLECTION. On what do you base your assurance of salvation? What have you learned from your study of Hebrews that has given you hope, encouragement and strength for your faith race?

In the concluding chapter, the writer to the Hebrews sketches a variety of duties to God and humanity. Together they reveal an exalted level of personal morality and duty. *Read Hebrews 13.*

---

1. Verses 1-3 tie in with verse 16. What actions are described here?

In what sense should these actions be considered "sacrifices" to God?

2. Sexual purity is one of God's absolutes (v. 4). How do you account for sexual impurity among professing Christians?

3. What facts about God help keep you from loving money (vv. 5-6)?

4. Obligations to spiritual leaders are laid out in verses 7, 17-18. What is here that we should follow?

How can you do this in your church?

5. For their part, what should spiritual leaders be doing?

6. Suppose someone challenged you to prove the flat claim of verse 8. Based on Hebrews, what would you say?

7. The writer cannot resist another magnificent portrait of Jesus, again set against the backdrop of the old system (vv. 9-10). What new application is made of Jesus' suffering, and which teachings have you encountered before in Hebrews (vv. 13-14)?

8. In what sense is our praise a sacrifice to God (v. 15)?

9. What insights do you gain about the writer (vv. 18-19, 22-25)?

10. Verses 20-21 are a benediction, a summary prayer. In making it a personal prayer, what kind of "equipment" would you ask God for? Why?

11. On the basis of your study of Hebrews, what do you think God would like to "work" in you that would please him?

Allow thoughts of praise and thanksgiving to fill your mind and heart. Give your will to Christ. Ask him to enable you to keep all of the injunctions in this chapter.

Now or Later

Think about your major impressions of Hebrews. What do you think is the "big idea" of the book?

How has it changed your thinking as well as your approach to Christian living, worship and service?

Leader's Notes

Leading a Bible discussion can be an enjoyable and rewarding experience. But it can also be *scary*—especially if you've never done it before. If this is your feeling, you're in good company. When God asked Moses to lead the Israelites out of Egypt, he replied, "O Lord, please send someone else to do it"! (Ex 4:13). It was the same with Solomon, Jeremiah and Timothy, but God helped these people in spite of their weaknesses, and he will help you as well.

You don't need to be an expert on the Bible or a trained teacher to lead a Bible discussion. The idea behind these inductive studies is that the leader guides group members to discover for themselves what the Bible has to say. This method of learning will allow group members to remember much more of what is said than a lecture would.

These studies are designed to be led easily. As a matter of fact, the flow of questions through the passage from observation to interpretation to application is so natural that you may feel that the studies lead themselves. This study guide is also flexible. You can use it with a variety of groups—student, professional, neighborhood or church groups. Each study takes forty-five to sixty minutes in a group setting.

There are some important facts to know about group dynamics and encouraging discussion. The suggestions listed below should enable you to effectively and enjoyably fulfill your role as leader.

Preparing for the Study

1. Ask God to help you understand and apply the passage in your own life. Unless this happens, you will not be prepared to lead others. Pray too for the various members of the group. Ask God to open your hearts to the message of his Word and motivate you to action.

2. Read the introduction to the entire guide to get an overview of the entire book and the issues which will be explored.

3. As you begin each study, read and reread the assigned Bible passage to familiarize yourself with it.

4. This study guide is based on the New International Version of the Bible. It will help you and the group if you use this translation as the basis for your study and discussion.

5. Carefully work through each question in the study. Spend time in meditation and reflection as you consider how to respond.

6. Write your thoughts and responses in the space provided in the study guide. This will help you to express your understanding of the passage clearly.

7. It might help to have a Bible dictionary handy. Use it to look up any unfamiliar words, names or places. (For additional help on how to study a passage, see chapter five of *How to Lead a LifeBuilder Bible Study*, IVP, 2018.)

8. Consider how you can apply the Scripture to your life. Remember that the group will follow your lead in responding to the studies. They will not go any deeper than you do.

9. Once you have finished your own study of the passage, familiarize yourself with the leader's notes for the study you are leading. These are designed to help you in several ways. First, they tell you the purpose the study guide author had in mind when writing the study. Take time to think through how the study questions work together to accomplish that purpose. Second, the notes provide you with additional background information or suggestions on group dynamics for various questions. This information can be useful when people have difficulty understanding or answering a question. Third, the leader's notes can alert you to potential problems you may encounter during the study.

10. If you wish to remind yourself of anything mentioned in the leader's notes, make a note to yourself below that question in the study.

Leading the Study

1. Begin the study on time. Open with prayer, asking God to help the group to understand and apply the passage.

2. Be sure that everyone in your group has a study guide. Encourage the group to prepare beforehand for each discussion by reading the introduction to the guide and by working through the questions in the study.

3. At the beginning of your first time together, explain that these studies are meant to be discussions, not lectures. Encourage the members of the group to participate. However, do not put pressure on those who may be hesitant to speak during the first few sessions. You may want to suggest the following guidelines to your group.

☐ Stick to the topic being discussed.

☐ Your responses should be based on the verses which are the focus of the discussion and not on outside authorities such as commentaries or speakers.

☐ These studies focus on a particular passage of Scripture. Only rarely should you refer to other portions of the Bible. This allows for everyone to participate in in-depth study on equal ground.

☐ Anything said in the group is considered confidential and will not be discussed outside the group unless specific permission is given to do so.

☐ We will listen attentively to each other and provide time for each person present to talk.

☐ We will pray for each other.

4. Have a group member read the introduction at the beginning of the discussion.

5. Every session begins with a group discussion question. The question or activity is meant to be used before the passage is read. The question introduces the theme of the study and encourages group members to begin to open up. Encourage as many members as possible to participate, and be ready to get the discussion going with your own response.

This section is designed to reveal where our thoughts or feelings need to be transformed by Scripture. That is why it is especially important not to read the passage before the discussion question is asked. The passage will tend to color the honest reactions people would otherwise give because they are, of course, supposed to think the way the Bible does.

You may want to supplement the group discussion question with an ice-breaker to help people to get comfortable. See the community section of the *Small Group Starter Kit* (IVP, 1995) for more ideas.

You also might want to use the personal reflection question with your group. Either allow a time of silence for people to respond individually or discuss it together.

6. Have a group member (or members if the passage is long) read aloud the passage to be studied. Then give people several minutes to read the passage again silently so that they can take it all in.

7. Question 1 will generally be an overview question designed to briefly survey the passage. Encourage the group to look at the whole passage, but try to avoid getting sidetracked by questions or issues that will be addressed later in the study.

8. As you ask the questions, keep in mind that they are designed to be used just as they are written. You may simply read them aloud. Or you may prefer to express them in your own words.

There may be times when it is appropriate to deviate from the study guide. For example, a question may have already been answered. If so, move on to the next question. Or someone may raise an important question not covered in the guide. Take time to discuss it, but try to keep the group from going off on tangents.

9. Avoid answering your own questions. If necessary, repeat or rephrase them until they are clearly understood. Or point out something you read in the leader's notes to clarify the context or meaning. An eager group quickly becomes passive and silent if they think the leader will do most of the talking.

10. Don't be afraid of silence. People may need time to think about the question before formulating their answers.

11. Don't be content with just one answer. Ask, "What do the rest of you think?" or "Anything else?" until several people have given answers to the question.

12. Acknowledge all contributions. Try to be affirming whenever possible. Never reject an answer. If it is clearly off-base, ask, "Which verse led you to that conclusion?" or again, "What do the rest of you think?"

13. Don't expect every answer to be addressed to you, even though this will probably happen at first. As group members become more at ease, they will begin to truly interact with each other. This is one sign of healthy discussion.

14. Don't be afraid of controversy. It can be very stimulating. If you don't resolve an issue completely, don't be frustrated. Move on and keep it in mind for later. A subsequent study may solve the problem.

15. Periodically summarize what the group has said about the passage. This helps to draw together the various ideas mentioned and gives continuity to the study. But don't preach.

16. At the end of the Bible discussion you may want to allow group members a time of quiet to work on an idea under "Now or Later." Then discuss what you experienced. Or you may want to encourage group members to work on these ideas between meetings. Give an opportunity during the session for people to talk about what they are learning.

17. Conclude your time together with conversational prayer, adapting the prayer suggestion at the end of the study to your group. Ask for God's help in following through on the commitments you've made.

18. End on time.

Many more suggestions and helps are found in *How to Lead a LifeBuilder Bible Study*.

Components of Small Groups

A healthy small group should do more than study the Bible. There are four components to consider as you structure your time together.

Nurture. Small groups help us to grow in our knowledge and love of God. Bible study is the key to making this happen and is the foundation of your small group.

Community. Small groups are a great place to develop deep friendships with other Christians. Allow time for informal interaction before and after each study. Plan activities and games that will help you get to know each other. Spend time having fun together—going on a picnic or cooking dinner together.

Worship and prayer. Your study will be enhanced by spending time praising God together in prayer or song. Pray for each other's needs—and keep track of how God is answering prayer in your group. Ask God to help you to apply what you are learning in your study.

Outreach. Reaching out to others can be a practical way of applying what you are learning, and it will keep your group from becoming self-focused. Host a series of evangelistic discussions for your friends or neighbors. Clean up the yard of an elderly friend. Serve at a soup kitchen together, or spend a day working in the community.

Many more suggestions and helps in each of these areas are found in the *Small Group Starter Kit.* You will also find information on building a small group. Reading through the starter kit will be worth your time.

Study 1. Hebrews 1. Starting the Race.

Purpose: To gain a firm grasp of who Jesus Christ really is.

Group Discussion. Every study begins with a question that is meant to be asked before the passage is read. These questions are important for several reasons.

First, they help the group to warm up to each other. No matter how well a group may know each other, there is always a stiffness that needs to be overcome before people will begin to talk openly. A good question will break the ice.

Second, approach questions get people thinking along the lines of the topic of the study. Most people will have lots of different things going on in their minds (dinner, an important meeting coming up, how to get the car fixed) that will have nothing to do with the study. A creative question will get their attention and draw them into the discussion.

Third, approach questions can reveal where our thoughts or feelings need to be transformed by Scripture. That is why it is especially important not to read the passage before the approach question is asked. The passage will tend to color the honest reactions people would otherwise give because they are, of course, supposed to think the way the Bible does. Giving honest responses before they find out what the Bible says may help them see where their thoughts or attitudes need to be changed.

Personal Reflection. These ideas are designed for those who want to have a more meditative or devotional experience. If you are leading a group, you could also allow a time of silence for members to pray or reflect as they come into God's presence.

Question 1. These verses show that Jesus supersedes the earlier mediators between God and humanity—the prophets. "In these last days" (v. 2) was used by Hebrew prophets to denote when their words would be fulfilled. The appearance of Jesus inaugurates this time of fulfillment.

Question 3. "Radiance" (v. 3) means the visible outshining of God's glory. Christ's brightness is of the same substance as the source of light. "Exact representation of his being" (v. 3) means an exact expression of the divine nature, the very image of the substance of God, just like the image on a coin exactly corresponds to the mold from which it is cast.

Question 4. Christ's work of purification of sins (v. 3) will emerge as a major emphasis of the writer in chapters 9-10. Christ's role in purifying our sins assumes greater prominence than his work as Creator, for example, because of Christ's role as our great high priest. In God's redemptive plan it was not by creation that Jesus saved us, but by his death and resurrection.

Question 5. "The right hand of the Majesty in heaven" (v. 3) does not mean either a physical right hand or a material throne. The language denotes Christ's exaltation and supremacy.

Question 6. The writer's application of the facts of verses 1-3 surprises us because proving Christ's superiority to angels (v. 4) is not a priority for us. This was important to the Hebrews, steeped as they were in angel worship (13:9; Col 2:18), probably because of angelic visitations to their Old Testament forebears.

For example, Christ's better names, "Son" (v. 5) and "firstborn" (v. 6), are titles of uncreated deity. Jesus is addressed as God (v. 8) and shows his deity by his righteous kingdom rule. One day all of his enemies will be vanquished (v. 13).

Question 8. If you feel it's needed, you might ask, "Who is the source of all of these astounding statements?" (vv. 5-8, 10, 13) to draw out the role of God's authority. Help the group to recognize how this New Testament use of Old Testament Scripture makes it possible for today's Christians to see the significance of Christ in the Old Testament.

Study 2. Hebrews 2. Warning Signs.

Purpose: To be aware of and act to protect ourselves from the danger of spiritual drifting.

Question 1. "What we have heard" (v. 1) would refer immediately to the supremacy of Jesus in chapter 1. More broadly, it includes the total message of the gospel about Jesus Christ by which the Hebrews had become Christians.

Question 2. It is possible to drift intellectually: "I used to believe that." One can drift morally: "I used to think those things were wrong." One can drift from worship, Bible reading, witness and service: "I can't find time for those things anymore." For the Hebrews, their immediate danger was drifting from commitment to Christ back into Judaism.

"The message spoken by angels" refers to the giving of the Mosaic Law on Mount Sinai (see, for example, Acts 7:53; Gal 3:19).

Question 3. What is the "just punishment" for those who drift away from and ignore their "great salvation"? The writer does not describe it. But the author is so fearful of the prospect that the readers are urged as strongly as possible to keep on in their faith race. See, for example, Paul's warnings: "Continue to work out your salvation with fear and trembling" (Phil 2:12). "Examine yourselves to see whether you are in the faith; test yourselves" (2 Cor 13:5).

Some commentators and scholars interpret these warning passages as referring to ultimate questions of salvation. "Just punishment," according to this view, refers to eternal suffering in hell.

On the other hand, in Hebrews 3:14, the author gives the example of the Israelites who perished in the wilderness because of their unbelief (1 Cor 10:1-5). This suggests that God's "just punishment" of those who drift away is carried out in this life. We can't be sure of what it may be, but Paul warns of sickness and death (1 Cor 11:27-32). Because of the "here and now" example of God's judgment on drifters (his children in the wilderness), and because the writer does not mention heaven and hell as the specific issue for these people, I take it that the punishment is both physical and spiritual. This could mean loss of life or something equivalent, or what could be worse, loss of God's blessing and all the advantages of Christ's ever-present help in this life.

If we neglect Jesus, we miss out on the best God has to offer us now. The Hebrews had confessed their faith in Jesus. They were Christian believers. But the peril they faced was turning away from him under pressure and reverting to Old Testament Judaism, especially angel worship. This is a real and present pressure today for converts to Christianity from other religious systems, ancient (Hinduism, Buddhism, Islam) and modern (Mormonism, Christian Science, New Age and so on).

Question 6. To prove that Jesus is our merciful and faithful high priest, and

thus able to help us no matter what, the author shows that he temporarily
was lower than angels (v. 7), shared our flesh and blood (v. 14), and was
made like us (v. 17). Jesus "was made a little lower than the angels" (v. 9)
temporarily, while he voluntarily became flesh and blood to suffer death for
us. Paradoxically, he was raised to the place of highest exaltation.

Question 7. The perfect Son of God has become our perfect Savior (v. 10),
opening the way to God. In order to accomplish that, he must endure suffering and death. The path we tread he must first tread as our leader to God.
Only such a perfect Leader can be our adequate representative in God's presence.

Question 8. Jesus was born in the line of Abraham's physical descendants,
but in verse 16 Abraham's seed is the whole family of Christian believers.

Question 9. The Hebrews were tempted to be disloyal to God and to give up
their Christian profession.

Study 3. Hebrews 3. Winning the Race.

Purpose: To understand the factors that make for spiritual success or failure.

Question 1. "Therefore" (v. 1) refers to the gracious offer of Jesus to help us
when we are tempted, which is described in 2:18. The tragic fate of the Israelites who perished in the desert serves as the basis of God's warning to us.

Question 2. Both Moses and Christ were sent by God to lead the people—
"the one to lead them from bondage under Pharaoh to the promised land, the
other to lead them from bondage under the devil (2:14-15) to the Sabbath-
rest promised to those who believe (4:3, 9)" (*The NIV Study Bible*, ed. Ken-
neth Barker [Grand Rapids, Mich.: Zondervan, 1985], p. 1861).

Question 4. The example given is taken from Psalm 95:7-11, which focuses
on the generation that rebelled and perished in the wilderness. For an idea of
how the Israelites rebelled in the wilderness, read Numbers 11:1, 4-6, 31-33;
13:30—14:3, 19-24, 32-35. It is important to recognize that their unbelief
was not a lack of belief in God, but questioning God's way and lacking trust
in him. Their unbelief was plain disobedience to God. In these verses we also
see that Caleb was a brother who held fast.

Question 8. God's "rest" (vv. 11, 18) was the Promised Land of Canaan, not
heaven. It was the place of present enjoyment of God's richest blessings.
However, some would say that the promise of rest in Canaan points to the
eternal rest we find in salvation.

Question 11. Keep in mind that both God's blessing and judgment of these
brothers in the race are present, not future (that is, not heaven and hell). The
essential belief in God's work through Christ is present in the brothers. Also

see the leader's note on study 2, question 3.

Study 4. Hebrews 4:1-13. Receiving God's Blessings.
Purpose: To anticipate the joy of striving for God's best.
Question 1. God's rest is illustrated by his rest after his creation work. His rest is shared by those who believe and obey him. It comes from a personal knowledge of Jesus Christ (see, for example, Mt 11:28-30; Jn 7:37-39; 10:10; 14:23, 27; 15:11; 16:33; Eph 3:16-19; Phil 4:6-7; 1 Pet 5:7, 10-11). Entering God's rest now means death to self, all our self-goodness. Evan Hopkins prayed about rest in this way: "My Saviour, thou hast offered rest; Oh, give it then to me; The rest of ceasing from myself; To find my all in thee."
Question 4. Faith and obedience go hand in hand. If you say you believe, you must obey God. Faith that grasps God's opportunities is genuine, persistent and continuing, not just hearing the message and saying, "Yes, I believe it."
Question 5. Be careful to avoid arguments about Saturday or Sunday being the day to rest. Deal practically with the larger principles: (1) how to cease from trying to please God to earn salvation and (2) how to enjoy God's deliverance in Christ, which offers freedom from the tyranny of work. Ask the group to find applications to both spiritual and physical rest, especially when the demands of work often crowd out worship, witness and service.
Question 6. According to Moses, the people knew that the land west of the Jordan was to be a place of peace and rest (Deut 12:9-10).
Question 7. Be sure to guard the context here so as not to stray from the writer's main point. Our failure to achieve God's promised rest relates directly to our lack of faith.
Question 8. Encourage stories about how God does this through reading, study, preaching and teaching.

Study 5. Hebrews 4:14—5:10. Overcoming Weakness.
Purpose: To find hope in Christ's high priesthood in the face of temptation.
Question 1. Allow ample time for a cursory review of the facts, but do not explore the interpretation at this point. Subsequent questions will explore their meaning and application.
Question 4. God's mercy and grace are guaranteed because Jesus withstood the trials of our weaknesses without sin. Therefore, he is our effective mediator between us and God.
Question 5. The Old Testament accounts are found in Exodus 28:1, Leviticus 9:7 and 16:6. It was vital for the Hebrew Christians to see this link with their

past religious traditions.

Question 6. The author shows that Jesus' priesthood was chosen by God; he did not take it upon himself. Jesus has this in common with Jewish high priests. But of no earthly high priest did God say, "You are my son," thus showing Christ's divine appointment.

Question 9. Jesus "learned obedience" not in the sense that he was a disobedient son, but in his suffering he learned the full meaning and cost of his obedience. You might want to look at one account of his Passion in Matthew 26:36-49.

Don't worry about Melchizedek (5:6, 10) now. We'll meet him again in chapter 7.

Study 6. Hebrews 5:11—6:20. The Race to Maturity.

Purpose: To gain a new aspiration for spiritual maturity.

Question 4. Certain basics of our Christian faith must be self-evident: faith, resurrection, repentance and judgment. It is not clear what the writer meant by "instruction about baptisms" and "the laying on of hands."

Question 5. The benefit of Christ's sacrifice is "once for all." According to one interpretation of 6:4-6, anyone who has shared in the grace of Christ and then rejects the gospel (without, of course, ever truly believing) cannot be brought again to repentance and faith. Or another possibility is that the verse is describing a person who has truly believed the gospel and then turned away from it and lived as though the gospel makes no difference. Such a person also cannot be brought again to life-changing faith. Even to suggest that Jesus be crucified again (v. 6) is unthinkable. A second repentance is impossible, just as it was for the disobedient Israelites in the wilderness. Whatever view you take, the nature of this danger amounts to a rejection of the saving work of Christ. The person is in extreme peril.

Question 6. We might picture here a runner falling beside the track or a child giving up a hard task. For the Hebrews, this would mean abandoning their faith. Or to follow previous descriptions it would result in drift and neglect (2:1-3), hardness of heart (3:12-19), missing God's rest (4:1-2, 11-13), and spiritual infancy and dullness instead of maturity (5:11-14). They were in danger of passing the point of no return, where it would be impossible to start over, as was the case with the Israelites in the wilderness. Only God knows when a person's persistent disobedience brings such judgment. He pulled down the curtain on the Israelites after repeated provocations.

Question 7. For other facts about God's judgment of the "produce" of our lives, see Romans 4:10-12; 1 Corinthians 3:9-15; 2 Corinthians 5:9-10.

Question 10. In 6:13 the writer returns to his theological discussion (4:14—5:10). This theme of God's promise, sealed by Christ's atoning death, will be pursued by comparing it with the old system of Jewish sacrifices.

Question 12. The veil of the temple in Jerusalem guarded the inner sanctuary, the holy of holies, which was entered only once a year by the high priest.

Study 7. Hebrews 7. Eternal Companion.

Purpose: To develop new levels of confidence in Jesus Christ.

Question 1. Melchizedek was a king and a priest (Gen 14:18). Obviously he had parents and he died. What the writer is saying is that there is no record of his birth or death, so it is as if he had no beginning or ending. He is thus a prototype of Christ, our eternal high priest.

Question 2. The writer emphasizes Melchizedek's priesthood by reporting that Abraham gave him the tithe of his best booty, and in return he received the blessing. In two ways he showed he was inferior to the priest. The Levites were superior to all other Jews because they collected the tithe. But Levi, through Abraham, paid the tithe to Melchizedek. The writer's purpose in reciting these details is to prove Christ's superiority.

Question 3. Perfection (v. 11) refers to our ability to draw near to God (vv. 7:19; 9:9; 10:22). Jesus descended from Judah (v. 14), but he was nevertheless destined to be a priest. Christ's authority as priest depended on his resurrection (v. 16).

Question 5. Basically, the rules and regulations did not bring anyone to maturity. A runner won't go on to maturity by learning the rules of track and field alone. A better hope is needed to bring people to maturity.

Question 7. The new covenant is neither provisional nor temporary. It is permanent, and it is effective. God's plan to forgive sins and to bring people into fellowship with himself will be carried out.

Question 10. The writer climaxes this section on Christ's superiority to the former priesthood. Jesus guarantees a better covenant (v. 22). The covenant is only as permanent as the priesthood. Therefore, Jesus is the only one who can save us.

Study 8. Hebrews 8. God's "New Deal."

Purpose: To gain new appreciation of God's love and mercy in his new covenant.

Question 2. Jesus offered himself (v. 3; see also 7:27; 9:14; 10:10). His offering was accomplished and finished in one decisive act. The act of offering doesn't continue. The fact that Jesus' one offering was accepted by God as eternally sufficient for us and our sins is proven by the fact that Jesus is permanently enthroned in the place of all power (10:12-13).

Question 4. When God promised a new covenant to the prophet Jeremiah (which is quoted in Heb 8:8-12), he indicated that the first covenant failed because the Israelites failed to abide by its conditions. The agreement itself, though genuine and good, provided no way for sinful people to continue to be faithful to God.

Question 5. The ultimate fulfillment of these promises awaits the return of Jesus to reign on the earth. For example, it is not yet true that everyone knows the Lord (v. 11). But here we have a very clear picture of what Jesus wants to do now for everyone who professes faith in him.

Question 6. God's plan means a change away from the law as an external restraint, from which people often break away, to an inner constraint. This change is accomplished by putting the Spirit of obedience in our hearts, so that like Jesus himself we will say, "I desire to do your will, O my God; your law is within my heart" (Ps 40:8). The whole point of this change is to give us a direct, personal knowledge of God himself.

Question 10. The foundation of God's mercy is Christ's high priestly work of putting away sin. This makes it possible for us to draw near to God. Therefore, Jesus is the mediator of the new covenant with its better promises (v. 6).

Question 11. Allow people to reflect. Possible responses might include a release from guilt, freedom from fear of future judgment or eagerness to make a fresh start with God.

Study 9. Hebrews 9. The Runner's Power.

Purpose: To find in Jesus' sacrifice of himself a strong, secure foundation for life.

Question 2. The writer summarizes how God's plan for sacrifices in the Old Testament was carried out under ideal conditions. The rules are fully described in Exodus 25—26.

Question 3. According to the laws of Moses, only the high priest was permitted to enter the innermost sanctuary beyond the second curtain. First, he atoned for his own and his family's sins (Lev 16).

Question 4. The new covenant brought reformation with Christ as high priest. Note what he offered (v. 12), where he made his offering (vv. 11-12), how often (v. 12) and with what results (vv. 12-14).

The second part of this question requires some careful thought about facts that may be unfamiliar to some people. It also requires some knowledge of the Old Testament sacrificial system. The discussion should highlight the main points of the writer's case for the superiority of Christ's sacrifice.

Question 5. Allow time for careful reflection. This may be difficult because we do not ordinarily think in these theological terms. Aim to make the answers relevant to real-life circumstances.

Question 6. God's new agreement is compared to a human will, or testament, which becomes effective only after the testator's death. Similarly, the new covenant becomes effective by Christ's death. Because sin brings death, the blood of thousands of animals was required under Old Testament law. Under the new covenant the blood of Jesus is required. God's just and righteous judgment must be satisfied. There is no forgiveness, no salvation apart from the shedding of blood.

Question 7. Give people time to talk about why heavenly facts do not usually absorb us. What disciplines are required of us if we are to think more about Jesus in heaven?

Question 10. Encourage people to talk about ideas that have worked for them.

Study 10. Hebrews 10. Staying in the Race.
Purpose: To develop stronger relations with Christ and with fellow believers.

Question 1. The law does not lead to salvation. Its inferiority in dealing with sin is proved because it demands repeated sacrifices.

Question 2. Verses 5-7 are quoted as the words of Jesus. They are based on the Greek version of the Old Testament (Septuagint), taken from Psalm 40:6-8. In Christ's sacrifice the terms of the old covenant were wiped out. God's people are now consecrated for true obedience.

Question 5. Many Christians worry about their feelings, which go up and down like a roller coaster. Many things affect our feelings, not all of them having to do with our faith race. On the other hand, Scripture teaches that unconfessed sin breaks our fellowship with God. We can get help when we're feeling down by praying with other believers and talking with more mature Christians.

Question 6. Beginning at 10:19, the writer launches into exhortations to live as faithful believers. Old Testament theology and the doctrines about Christ's superiority laid the foundation for teaching about how we should live. The new covenant provided by Christ's sacrifices shapes the behavior of God's people. Behavior follows belief, Christian conduct follows Christian confession.

Question 8. Encourage fresh examples of helping one another to follow Christ. Look for common factors in the stories.

Question 10. God's judgment of Christians is both present punishment (as was the case of the Israelites who perished in the wilderness) and future evaluation of their lives and service at the judgment seat of Christ (1 Cor 3:10-17).

Study 11. Hebrews 11. Models of Faith.
Purpose: To emulate the heroes and heroines of faith.

Question 6. "He as good as dead" (v. 12) refers to Abraham's advanced age (ninety-nine) when Isaac was born.

Question 9. While today's world calls survivors heroes, Hebrews makes clear that those who perished were also heroes and heroines of faith.

Question 10. Perhaps some people in your group have been influenced by the so-called prosperity gospel. The implication of this teaching is that if a Christian goes through a hard time, he or she lacks faith. The idea is contrary to the New Testament, which teaches that suffering is to be expected by Christians, who can glorify God in their suffering.

Question 11. "Better resurrection" in verse 35 refers to the resurrection life. The Revised Standard Version translates the second half of the verse "Some were tortured, refusing to accept release, that they might rise again to a better life."

Question 12. Encourage the group to make this question personal by citing something faith in God has given them or enabled them to do in life.

Study 12. Hebrews 12. The Runner's Discipline.
Purpose: To appreciate and grow by the values of God's discipline.

Question 1. Encourage honesty. Avoid vague generalities, but don't embarrass anyone.

Question 3. We should keep our eyes on Jesus in the way a runner focuses on the finish line. Our faith has both its beginning and completion in him. Jesus is also the supreme example as one who has already completed the race.

Question 4. The writer of Hebrews was focusing on the persecution—flogging, imprisonment—that the Christians were facing.

Questions 5-6. The writer discusses discipline in the family setting (verses 7-10). Then he returns to the analogy of athletic training (verses 1-2, 11-13).

Question 8. This aspect of Christian living is not often identified as a hindrance in our faith race. Be prepared with some examples to make it clear. For more information on Esau read Genesis 25:29-34. Esau gave up his birthright in exchange for a meal.

Question 9. Verses 18-29 return to the Old Testament picture of worship. The writer shows how the true worship of God is empowered by the new covenant, not the old.

Study 13. Hebrews 13. Running by the Rules.

Purpose: To find new ways to please God through our behavior.

General note. Note that verses 19 and 23 suggest that the writer was in prison and that Timothy also had been in prison.

Question 1. Notice "loving others, doing good, sharing, entertaining strangers, and helping the prisoners and the mistreated people."

Question 2. Do not allow this to become a gossip session or a collection of "can you top this?" stories. It is unwholesome to wallow in stories about sexual failures.

Question 3. When materialism and material goals threaten to overwhelm us, and many people are deeply in credit card debt, it's good to give some thought to the relation between our faith and our money.

Question 4. This is not the place to debate which church procedures are right and which ones are wrong. Regardless of the form of church government, there are some basic principles here for church leaders.

Question 7. To receive the benefits of Christ's sacrifice for our sins, the Hebrews had to abandon the "camp" (v. 13), that is, the abode of unbelieving Israel, with its old laws and rules. In effect they had to share the reproach and rejection of Jesus himself by Israel (Jn 1:11; Acts 5:30, 41).

Question 11. Plan to budget your discussion time so you get to this important opportunity to review Hebrews.

James Reapsome was a pastor and editor of the Evangelical Missions Quarterly *and* World Pulse Newsletter. *He was the author or coauthor of the other LifeBuilder Studies* Exodus, Grief, Marriage *and* Songs from Scripture.